Lake District

Lake District

Roland Smith

Waterton Press Limited

First published in the United Kingdom in 1998 by
Frith Publishing an imprint of Waterton Press Limited.

British Library Cataloguing in Publication Data.

Roland Smith
Lake District

ISBN 1-84125-029-5

Reproductions of all the photographs in this book are available as framed or mounted prints. For more information please contact The Francis Frith Collection at the address below quoting the title of this book and the page number and photograph number or title.

The Francis Frith Collection,
PO Box 1697, Salisbury, Wilts SP3 5TW
Tel: 01747 855 669
E mail: bookprints@francisfrith.com
Web pages: www.francisfrith.com

Typeset in Bembo

Printed and bound in Great Britain by
WBC Limited, Bridgend, Glamorgan.

Contents

Francis Frith 1822–1898

Introduction
Francis Frith
A Victorian Pioneer

Francis Frith, the founder of the world famous photographic archive was a complex and multitudinous man. A devout Quaker and a highly successful and respected Victorian businessman he was also a flamboyant character.

By 1855 Frith had already established a wholesale grocery business in Liverpool and sold it for the astonishing sum of £200,000, equivalent of over £15,000,000 today. Now a multi-millionaire he was able to indulge in his irresistible desire to travel. As a child he had poured over books penned by early explorers, and his imagination had been stirred by family holidays to the sublime mountain regions of Wales and Scotland. "What a land of spirit-stirring and enriching scenes and places!" he had written. He was to return to these scenes of grandeur in later years to "recapture the thousands of vivid and tender memories", but with a very different purpose. Now in his thirties, and captivated by the new science of photography, Frith set out on a series of pioneering journeys to the Middle East, that occupied him from 1856 until 1860.

He took with him a specially-designed wicker carriage which acted as camera, dark-room and sleeping chamber. These far-flung journeys were full of intrigue and adventure. In his life story, written when he was sixty-three, Frith tells of being held captive by bandits, and fighting "an awful midnight battle to the very point of exhaustion and surrender with a deadly pack of hungry, wild dogs". He bargained for several weeks with a "mysterious priest" over a beautiful seven-volume illuminated Koran, which is now in the British Museum. Wearing full arab costume, Frith arrived at Akaba by camel seventy years before Lawrence of Arabia, where he encountered "desert princes and rival sheikhs, blazing with jewel-hilted swords".

During these extraordinary adventures he was assiduously exploring the desert regions of the nile and recording the antiquities and people with his camera, Frith was the first photographer ever to travel beyond the sixth cataract. Africa, we must remember, was still the "Dark Continent", and Stanley and Livingstone's famous meeting was a decade into the future. The conditions for picture taking confound belief. He laboured for hours on end in his dark-room in the sweltering heat, while the volatile collodion chemicals fizzed dangerously in their trays. Often he was forced to work in tombs and caves where conditions were cooler.

Back in London he exhibited his photographs and was "rapturously cheered" by the Royal

Society. His reputation as a photographer was made overnight. His photographs were issued in albums by James S. Virtue and William MacKenzie, and published simultaneously in London and New York. An eminent historian has likened their impact on the population of the time to that on our own generation of the first photographs taken on the surface of the moon.

Characteristically, Frith spotted the potential to create a new business as a specialist publisher of photographs. In 1860 he married Mary Ann Rosling and set out to photograph every city, town and village in Britain. For the next thirty years Frith travelled the country by train and by pony and trap, producing photographs that were keenly bought by the millions of Victorians who, because of the burgeoning rail network, were beginning to enjoy holidays and day trips to Britain's seaside resorts and beauty spots.

To meet the demand he gathered together a team of up to twelve photographers, and also published the work of independent artist-photographers of the reputation of Roger Fenton and Francis Bedford. Together with clerks and photographic printers he employed a substantial staff at his Reigate studios. To gain an understanding of the scale of Frith's business one only has to look at the catalogue issued by Frith & Co. in 1886. It runs to some 670 pages listing not only many thousands of views of the British Isles but also photographs of most major European countries, and China, Japan, the USA and Canada. By 1890 Frith had created the greatest specialist photographic publishing company in the world.

He died in 1898 at his villa in Cannes, his great project still growing. His sons, Eustace and Cyril, took over the task, and Frith & Co. continued in business for another seventy years, until by 1970 the archive contained over a third of a million pictures of 7,000 cities, towns and villages.

The photographic record he has left to us stands as a living monument to a remarkable and very special man.

Frith's dhow in Egypt *c.*1857

VILLAGES

Most of the larger villages and towns of the Lake District occupy the most favoured sites in the valley bottoms, or command important river crossings. Although small, many sites have the urban air of small townships, which is exactly what they were in the days when the grant of a right to hold a market made the settlement, however tiny, an important trading centre for the surrounding countryside.

NEWBY BRIDGE, 1914
A family group of children enjoy a boating trip on the River Leven at Newby Bridge, at the southern end of Windermere, in 1914. In the background is the sixteenth century five-arched bridge which gave the village its name.

TROUTBECK, *c*.1880
The name of this small settlement on the slopes of Wansfell Pike between Windermere and the Kirkstone Pass means exactly what it says – "the trout stream" – and it stands above a stream with the same name. At the south end of the village is Townend, a typical Lakeland statesman's house, now in the care of the National Trust.

EAMONT BRIDGE, 1893
Eamount Bridge, just south of Penrith on the A6, takes its name from this splendid three-arched bridge across the River Eamont. It is perhaps best known for its two prehistoric monuments: King Arthur's Round Table, a Bronze Age henge, and the former Neolithic stone circle and henge at Mayburgh, of which only one standing stone now remains.

Parish Church, CONISTON, 1926
The blue-grey slate walls of Coniston parish church looks down on a memorial to one of England's greatest writers and social reformers, John Ruskin. He lived for nearly 30 years at Brantwood, opposite the village on the eastern shore of the lake, and preferred to be buried here, rather than have a grander tomb in Westminster Abbey.

EAMONT BRIDGE, 1893

The proprietress of Taylforth's Hotel (left) in the main street of Eamont Bridge, stands outside to bid farewell to a guest departing in a pony and trap in this 1893 photograph. The photographer would certainly not be able to set up his tripod in the middle of the same street today!

CONISTON from the Church Tower, 1906

This 1906 view from the church tower at Coniston, looks towards the wooded slopes of High Guards and up the valley of the Yewdale Beck. The whitewashed cottages of the village cluster around the church where the Yewdale Beck enters to the western side of Coniston Water.

CONISTON, 1929

A pair of ramblers (right) heading for the hills, stride out purposefully past the Rayburne Hotel and café in the centre of Coniston village in 1929. The lack of traffic in the main street is in sharp contrast with the scene today in this busy little village in the south west Lakes.

AMBLESIDE from Loughrigg, 1892

This general view of Ambleside, at the northern end of Windermere, was taken from the slopes of Loughrigg Fell in 1892. The spire of the parish church watches over this bustling village which was founded in the fifteenth century, and once had thriving corn and bobbin mills on the River Rothay.

AMBLESIDE, from the gate, 1886

Another view of Ambleside, this time looking down on the village centre from, The Gate, towards the Rydal Fells. The fine Victorian buildings reflect the increased prosperity brought to the village by the tourist trade, which was just starting to burgeon at the time.

White Lion and Royal Oak Hotels, AMBLESIDE, 1912
The centre of Ambleside, showing Lamb's Royal Oak Hotel on the left and the White Lion Hotel, centre, in 1912. A coach-and-four has pulled up outside the White Lion, while bustle in the main street shows how busy Ambleside had become as a tourist centre by this time.

Queen's Hotel, AMBLESIDE, 1892
The umbrellas on the coach-and-four drawn up outside the ornate frontage of the Queen's Hotel, Ambleside, in this 1892 photograph, appear to have been raised to protect the holders from the sun, rather than the rain. Other coaches wait for their passengers outside the other hotels for a day on the lakes.

AMBLESIDE, 1912
Twenty years later, the coach and horses in the centre of Ambleside have been replaced by open motor cars and charabancs, as shown in this photograph taken in 1912.

Bridge House, AMBLESIDE, 1912
Easily the most famous, and photographed building in Ambleside, is Bridge House, a tiny one-up, one-down house constructed on a bridge over the Stock Beck. Originally built in the seventeenth century as the apple-store for Ambleside Hall, it is now a National Trust Information Centre.

Red Lion Square, GRASMERE, 1926

The Red Lion Hotel, on the right of the picture, gives its name to the square in the centre of the village, now dominated by traffic of a one-way system. The two cyclists meandering down the middle of the road would not be able to do so for long today!

Church Stile, GRASMERE, 1926

Church Stile is the name of the road which goes around the original thirteenth century parish church of St. Oswald in Grasmere, where there is a rare annual rush-bearing ceremony. Buried in the churchyard are William Wordsworth, his loving sister Dorothy, and the other members of the Wordsworth family.

Wordsworth's Cottage, GRASMERE, 1912
William Wordsworth lived with his sister, Dorothy, at Dove Cottage, just outside the village Grasmere, from 1799 to 1813, and wrote some of his best known poetry there. The cottage is now part of a museum dedicated to the life and work of the poet - the founder of the Lakeland Romantic Movement.

Rothay Hotel, Grasmere, 1912
Horse-drawn coaches and a motor car are drawn up outside the Rothay Hotel at Grasmere in this photograph taken in 1912. The fast-growing tourist trade made hotels such as this popular in the late nineteenth and earlier twentieth centuries.

HAWKSHEAD from Charity High, 1896
The south Lakeland village of Hawkshead, seen from the hill of Charity High, just outside the village, in 1896. Hawkshead is one of the prettiest Lakeland villages, standing at the head of Esthwaite Water and probably founded in the tenth century by Norseman called Haukr.

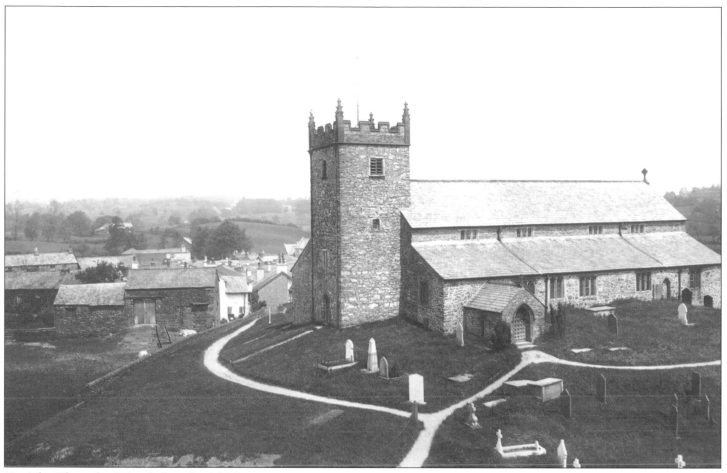

Parish Church, Hawkshead, 1892

The parish church of St. Michael's at Hawkshead, is one of the most interesting in the Lake District. Originally built as a chapel in the twelfth century, the present commanding building on its hill overlooking the village, mainly dates from the fifteenth century. It contains Tudor murals and painted texts on its walls, and its parish registers go back to the same period.

The Square, HAWKSHEAD, 1896

The picturesque cobbled square in the centre of Hawkshead, as it looked in 1896. An upended cart awaits its horse, while a little girl gazes across the empty square in anticipation. Now that most traffic by-passes this picturesque village, visitors can once again enjoy views like this, although it is seldom as quiet as this.

HAWKSHEAD, 1896
Shops waiting for the tourists in the centre of Hawkshead in 1896. The grey slate walls of the buildings and cobbled streets are typical of many Lakeland villages.

Flag Street, HAWKSHEAD, 1892
It is easy to see how this narrow Hawkshead street got its name, as it is paved by flagstones. The overhanging first-floor jetties of the whitewashed houses add to the medieval charm of the village, which is the favourite of the many visitors in the whole of the Lake District.

Bobbin Mill, HAWKSHEAD, 1896
Bobbin manufacture for the wool and cotton mills of the north of England was once an important industry in the well-wooded Lake District. Only 80 years ago, there were an estimated 25 bobbin mills, such as this one at Hawkshead photographed in 1896, still in production.

Old Grammer School House, HAWKSHEAD, 1929
The most famous student at Hawkshead Grammer School was William Wordsworth, who attended between 1779 and 1787. His initials can be seen carved in a desk there. The Grammer School was founded as long ago as 1585 and is open to the public today.

THE URBAN SCENE

In a predominately rural area such as the Lake District, there are few towns. The major ones actually within the Lake District are Kendal (see separate chapter), Keswick and Windermere. Other towns on the fringe of the district include Cockermouth and Penrith, and this collection of photographs covers the surprisingly urban aspect of the Lake Districts towns.

Keswick Bridge and Greta Hall, KESWICK, 1889
The bridge over the River Greta in the busy little market town of Keswick in the northern Lakes. In the distance, on the left of the picture, can just be seen Greta Hall, former home of the poets Samuel Taylor Coleridge and Robert Southey. The pencil works of A. Banks on the right, recalls one of Keswick's major industries, founded on supplies of plumbago or black lead from the Seathwaite valley in Borrowdale.

Parish Church, KESWICK, 1889
The elegant spire and pinnacles of the parish church of St. John's, Keswick, feature in many views of this town, at the foot of Skiddaw in the northern Lake District. The church was built in the nineteenth century on a slight hill, and also enjoys fine views over Derwent Water.

Riggs Hotel, WINDERMERE, 1929
Richard Rigg opened his Windermere Hotel in 1847 - the same year as the Kendal and Windermere Railway reached the town - and his yellow-and-black coaches provided a connecting service from the adjacent station to various parts of the Lake District. The hotel is now known as the Windermere Hotel.

The Promenade, BOWNESS, 1925
The provision of the public gardens of The Promenade at Bowness also followed the coming of the railway in 1847, and the increased popularity of the Lake District as a health-giving holiday resort for people from the industrial towns and cities of the north west.

Market Place, PENRITH, 1893
Penrith received its first market charter in 1223, and it has continued as a busy market town serving the north east of the Lake District and the North Pennines ever since. This view shows the Clock Tower and a surprisingly empty Market Place as it looked in 1893.

Cornmarket, PENRITH, *c*.1955
The Clock Tower in the previous picture can just be seen in the background of this 1950's photograph of Penrith's Cornmarket. Horse-drawn transport is obviously still in use, but about to be phased out by the motorised vehicles which were taking over the streets of the Cumbrian town.

King Street, PENRITH, 1960
Looking down Penrith's main shopping street – King Street – in 1960. The scene had not changed much since Victorian days, except for the fact that the horses had by now disappeared and have been replaced by motor vehicles.

Parish Church, PENRITH, 1893

The square red sandstone west tower of St. Andrew's Parish Church, Penrith, is Norman, and dates from the original church on the site. But the classical proportions of the rest of the church date from an extensive rebuilding in 1720. The whole building was restored by Sir A. Richardson in 1945. The Saxon crosses of the Giant's Grave are in the churchyard (see monuments and Houses).

Main Street, COCKERMOUTH, 1906

The clock Tower dominates the Main Street of the West Cumberland town of Cockermouth in this 1906 photograph. Cockermouth was granted its market charter in 1221, and gradually developed in importance until it was the chief commercial centre of the old county of Cumberland.

COCKERMOUTH, 1906
A general view of Cockermouth as it was in 1906. Cockermouth is situated where the River Cocker joins the River Derwent on its way to the Irish Sea at Workington. This view looks across the Workington-Cockermouth railway line, opened in 1847, towards the spire of the parish church of All Saints' on the right.

Wordsworth's Birthplace, COCKERMOUTH, *c.*1955
England's best known Romantic poet was born in this Georgian mansion in Cockermouth's Main Street in 1770. His father was steward to Sir James Lowther and moved to the house in 1766. The house overlooks the River Derwent and has a delightful garden and terrace. It is now in the care of the National Trust.

TRANSPORT

The first tourists to the Lake District arrived by coach-and-four, and the most usual form of local transport was packhorse or horse and cart. By the time this collection of photographs werc taken, the railway had arrived, but it was still to be many years before the Lakeland roads were to become choked with motor cars as they are today.

River Leven, Newby Bridge, 1914
Boating on the southern reaches of Windermere near Newby Bridge in 1914. This is still as popular pastime on Windermere - England's largest lake - and the calm reaches of the southern end of the lake provide a quiet backwater compared to the busy area around Bowness.

Sailing Boats on WINDERMERE, 1896
Organised sailing on Windermere started in the mid-nineteenth century. The Windermere Sailing Club, later to become the Royal Windermere Yacht Club, was founded in 1860 and organised regular regattas on the lake. This photograph, taken in 1896, shows a regatta in progress near Bowness-on-Windermere.

Bowness Ferry, WINDERMERE, 1896
The Bowness Ferry, across the narrowest part of the lake was originally a hand-rowed operation. But in 1870, twenty-six years before this photograph was taken, it became steam-operated and resulted in the building of The Ferry Hotel on the western shore in 1879. In this photograph, a charabanc is being transported across the lake by the chain-operated pulley ferry.

Bowness Ferry, WINDERMERE, 1896
Another view of the Bowness Ferry in 1896 shows a full coach-and-four just about to set out from the Bowness side of the lake, with the coachman at the front steadying the nervous horses. This must have been a special trip, because by this time, the sight of a coach-and-four was becoming increasingly rare.

Waterhead, WINDERMERE, 1912
Horse-drawn coaches wait patiently to take passengers from the boats at Waterhead, near Ambleside on Windermere, in 1912. The ornate Waterhead buildings served an increasing trade of tourists to the area, particularly after the railway came in 1847.

"Teal" at Bowness Pier, 1896
Packed to the gunwales, the newly-commissioned pleasure steamer *Teal* leaves Bowness Pier for a trip on Windermere in 1896. At this time, private boat ownership was beyond the means of all but the wealthiest visitors, so this was most people's only chance of enjoying the scenery from the lake.

Waterhead, CONISTON, 1912
Waterhead on Coniston Water has not changed significantly since this photograph was taken in 1912. Even the elegant steam cruiser the *Gondola,* seen here moored at the pier, is still taking passengers up and down the lake. Originally built in 1859, it was rescued as a rotting hulk and restored to public use by the National Trust in 1980.

Silecroft Station, *c.*1950
Carlisle and Sons's delivery van waits at the level crossing near Silecroft Station on the west coast route between Barrow and workington, which opened to traffic in 1848. Silecroft, near Millom stands at the southernmost extremity of the Lake District National Park, at the foot of Black Combe (1,970 ft).

Ravenglass & Eskdale Railway, ESKDALE GREEN, *c.*1950
The narrow-gauge Ravenglass & Eskdale Railway - affectionately known as "Lil' Ratty" - opened in 1875, to link iron mines in Eskdale to the main line at Ravenglass. Restoration by a group of railway enthusiasts led to its reopening in 1960, and it is now a major tourist attraction. This view was taken near Eskdale in the 1950's.

Hugh's Crag Bridge, PENRITH, 1893
Hugh's Crag Bridge on the Penrith to Cockermouth line in 1893. The line was opened in 1864 to link the iron industry of West Cumberland with coal from the West Durham coalfield, but it soon became popular with tourists visiting Keswick and the northern Lake District.

Newby Bridge Station, 1914
A steam train pulls into Newby Bridge Station, at the southern end of Windermere, in 1914. The Ulverston to Lakeside line was built in 1869, but closed and then reopened again in 1965 as a tourist railway, known as the Lakeside and Haverthwaite Railway.

MONUMENTS AND HOUSES

Probably because of its remoteness and lack of development, the Lake District is well-blessed with ancient monuments, from prehistoric stone circles and standing stones to the ruins of medieval castles. In addition, when the district became "fashionable" during the eighteenth and nineteenth centuries, the landed gentry chose it to build some of their most extravagent stately homes.

Long Meg near PENRITH, 1893
Long Meg and her Daughters, a Bronze Age stone circle near Little Salkeld is the largest in the Lake District, and one of the biggest in Britain. This photograph taken in 1893 shows a visitor staring wistfully at Long Meg herself - an "outlier" of the main, 59-stone circle. Just visible in the picture are faint spiral carvings which have been traced on the stone.

Castlerigg Stone Circle, 1895
Erroneously known in 1895 when this photograph was taken, as the Druid's Circle, the Castlerigg Stone Circle just outside Kewsick is dramatically set in an amphitheatre of hills, including Skiddaw, seen in the background (left). It is thought to date from the Neolithic or early Bronze Age periods, predating the Druids by many centuries.

Giant's Grave, Churchyard PENRITH,
The so-called "Giant's Grave" in the churchyard of St, Andrew at Penrith, is actually a pair of tall Norse-influenced Saxon crosses with two hog-backed grave slabs in between. Legend has it that this is the grave of Ewan Caesario, a giant who was King of Cumbria between 920 and 37 AD.

Kendal Castle, 1894
Kendal Castle was built by the Normans, probably by Ivo de Tailbois, the first Lord of Kendal in the late twelfth century, to the east of the town, and it still commands good views to the north and south-east. Katherine Parr, Henry VIII's sixth and surviving wife, was born here in 1512, but it was described as "ready to drop down with age" by the beginning of the seventeenth century.

Penrith Castle, 1893
Penrith Castle was built by William Strickland, later Bishop of Carlisle, who was given permission to build Penrith Castle in 1397, following the sacking of the town by raiding Scots in 1354. The curtain wall, shown in this 1893 photograph, is all that remains of Strickland's castle, which is now a public park.

Shap Abbey, 1893
Shap Abbey, near the banks of the River Lowther, was founded by the "white canons" of the Premonstratensian order at the end of the twelfth century, but it was dissolved like so many others in 1540. This 1893 photograph shows the imposing west tower, which was built about 1500, and which still stands almost to its full height.

Greystoke Castle, 1893
Like Lowther, Greystoke Castle near Penrith was built to show off the wealth of a local landowner, in this case Lord Greystoke. The architect Salvin incorporated the original fourteenth century pele tower in his 1840 reconstruction, executed in the style of an early seventeenth century mansion.

Holker Hall, 1894
The west wing of the original old hall at Holker, home of the Preston family since the sixteenth century, was destroyed by fire in 1871. This sumptuous rebuilding, supervised by the seventh Duke of Devonshire, was designed by Paley and Austin of Lancaster, and has been described as their most outstanding domestic work.

Eden Hall, PENRITH, 1893
The colonnaded front and formal gardens of Eden Hall, four miles east of Penrith, photographed in 1893. Demolished in the 1930's, Eden Hall stood on the site of an earlier medieval house built by Musgrave family. It was home to a legend concerning a 700-years-old glass cup which, while it was kept complete, would safeguard the future of the house.

Wray Castle and Boathouse, WINDERMERE, 1886
The stately Gothic pile of Wray Castle, Windermere, can just be seen peeping over the trees in the background of this 1886 photograph, taken near its boathouse on the lake. Wray Castle was built by Dr. James Dawson, a retired Liverpool surgeon, between 1840-7, and is one of the most extravagant of the nineteenth century Lake District mansions. It is now a Merchant Navy training college.

Brougham Castle, PENRITH, 1893

The imposing red sandstone ruins of the keep of Brougham Castle, near Penrith, watch over the River Eamont in this 1893 photograph. Brougham Castle was originally built by the Normans and strengthened by Henry II in 1170. This was one of many castles to which Lady Anne Clifford, Countess of Dorset, made improvements, and she died here at the age of 90 in 1678.

Cockermouth Castle, 1906

Cockermouth Castle was built in the thirteenth century on a strategic site to guard the confluence of the River Cocker and Derwent. Modifications, including a barbican and outer gatehouse, were made by Edward III in the fourteenth century, but the castle fell into ruin after a Civil War siege by Royalist forces in 1648.

Sizergh Castle, 1896
Inside the three-sided courtyard of Sizergh Castle, near Kendal, in 1896. Originally a fourteenth century defensive pele tower, Sizergh was home of the Strickland family, and the present building is mainly a fifteenth century Elizabethan mansion, now in the care of the National Trust.

Levens Hall Gardens, 1891

The magnificent topiary gardens of Levens Hall, near Kendal, were laid out by the King's gardener Beaumont, who trained at Versailles, in 1692. Levens Hall is a fine Elizabethan mansion built for the Bagot family around 1580, again around a fourteenth century pele tower.

THE RURAL SCENE

Outside the towns and villages of the Lake District, the rural scene had not changed much in many centuries. The small, isolated farmhouses and dalehead hamlets looked much as they had done since they were first established in the Middle Ages and before, as this selection of photographs shows.

BUTTERMERE, 1889
The hamlet at the foot of Buttermere in the western Lake District takes its name from the lake and is still the farming settlement as it has always been. This view, taken in 1889, looks up the lake towards the skyline peaks of Fleetwith Pike on the left and Haystacks on the right.

High Stile, BUTTERMERE, 1889
Buttermere takes its name from the Old English and means "the lake by the dairy pastures" - where the butter is made. The farmstead of High Stile, shown in this 1889 photograph, is still in the same business a thousand years later.

BUTTERMERE, 1889
Another view of the hamlet of Buttermere, taken in 1889. The small stock enclosure which goes across the Sail Beck was probably used for sheep washing in the summer, before shearing.

BUTTERMERE, *c.*1873
The hotel at Buttermere, formerly known as the Fish Hotel, was the scene in 1802 of a great scandal, when the daughter of the landlord, Mary Robinson or "the Maid of Buttermere", married a man who claimed to be a gentleman but who in fact was a fraudster, later hanged at Carlisle.

BORROWDALE, 1895
A hotel in Borrowdale, one of the wildest valleys in the Lakeland, in 1895. Early tourists were "horrified" at the expanses of naked rock and impending mountains of places like Borrowdale, and feared to travel far into the dale, until poets like Wordsworth popularised the "picturesque" mountain scenery.

GRANGE-IN-BORROWDALE, 1893
Grange is the hamlet at the foot of Borrowdale, where the River Derwent, seen on the left of this 1893 photograph, meanders through water meadows into mighty Derwent Water to the north. The name "grange" signifys an outlying farm, usually belonging to a monastery.

Wasdale Head Church, 1889

The tiny church of St Olaf at Wasdale Head, is said to be among the smallest in England. But surrounded by the dramatic mountains of Wasdale, it is also one of the most visited. There are many memorials in the 400-year-old building to walkers and climbers who have met their deaths on England's highest hills.

Victoria Hotel, WASTWATER, 1889

Wasdale and Wastwater can be said to have seen the birth of the sport of rock climbing, and climbers from all over Britain stayed at local hostelries such as the Victorian Hotel, Wastwater. Walter Haskett-Smith's first ascent of Napes Needle on Great Gable in 1886 - only three years before this photograph was taken - is widely held to be the advent of the sport.

Bowder Stone, BORROWDALE, 1893
The Bowder Stone, a 2,000-ton boulder which was transported to near Grange in Borrowdale by Ice Age glaciers, has been a source of tourist wonder for centuries. Today surrounded by trees, there is still a wooden staircase to reach the top, as seen in this 1893 photograph.

Scale Force, CRUMMOCK WATER, 1893.
Scale Force near Crummock Water is, at 172 ft the Lake District's longest waterfall. The path to the fall goes up from Buttermere village and the falls - in fact a series of cascades, are hidden in a tree-lined gorge.

Dungeon Ghyll Force, LANGDALE, 1888
These dramatic falls are hidden in the depths of Dungeon Ghyll in Great Langdale, and are seldom visited by car-bound tourists. The falls are caused by waters of the Dungeon Ghyll, which rises on the Langdale Pikes above, crashing through this tiny gorge of sheer-sided rocks.

Stepping Stones, AMBLESIDE, 1888
A crinoline-clad Victorian lady delicately picks her way across the Stepping Stones which cross the River Rothay, near Ambleside, in 1888. Ladies were not seen in walking trousers or breeches in those days!

Leven Estuary, GREENODD, 1921
Greenodd stands on the Leven Estuary where the River Leven from Windermere, and the River Crake from Coniston Water flow into Morecambe Bay and the Irish Sea. The line of the Furniss Railway, built in 1857, can be seen crossing the bay on the embankment to the right, in this 1921 photograph.

THE LAKES

It is the lakes which make the Lake District what it is, and they are what brings the majority of the tourists to the area. But there are several common misconceptions about them. There are actually only 16 lakes in the Lake District - and only one, Bassenthwaite, is actually called a lake. All the rest are "meres" or "waters", while the smaller mountain lakes are known as "tarns", but they were all originally formed in troughs gouged out of Ice Age glaciers.

WINDERMERE from Biskey How, 1887
The newly-built villas of Bowness-on-Windermere spread out towards the viewpoint of Biskey How in this 1887 view of the lake, looking towards the wooded island of Belle Isle, with the Claife Heights beyond.

WINDERMERE from Todd Crag, 1912
Looking south down the length of Windermere from Todd Crag, a southern outlier of Loughrigg Fell above the
hamlet of Clappersgate, in 1912. Immediately below the viewpoint, the River Rothay winds into England's
largest lake by Gale Naze Crag in the centre of the picture.

WINDERMERE, 1886
A farmer rests on a fence overlooking Windermere in this tranquil scene photographed in 1886. The wooden gates and fences in the photograph are typical of this southern, less-mountainous part of the Lake District, and the slightly-blurred leaves of the silver birch trees are caused by wind movement.

Nickle Landing Stage, WINDERMERE, 1914
A small boy in a rowing boat gazes at the reflection in the waters of the Windermere in this photograph taken during the summer of 1914. The location is the Nickle Landing Stage, near Newby Bridge, at the southern end of the lake, where it narrows to enter the River Leven.

WINDERMERE Ferry Boat, 1887
The original hand-rowed ferry service across the narrowest part of the Windermere at Bowness Nab. The lady in her long black dress and the gentleman wait for the ferryman to take them across to the western side of the lake, where the wooded Claife Heights stretch away to the right.

Waterside, Ambleside, WINDERMERE, 1912
A long line of rowing boats waiting for the customers stretch around the bay at Waterhead, near Ambleside on Windermere in this 1912 photograph. In the distance, Todd Crag and Loughrigg Fell fill in the left background.

Waterhead Hotel, WINDERMERE, 1887
Another view of Waterhead on Windermere, this time taken in 1887. It shows the Waterhead Hotel, built to serve the increasing numbers of tourists who were arriving by train at the Lakeside Station at Bowness, and catching a steamer up the lake to Waterhead.

BUTTERMERE, 1893
These elegant Scot's pines on the shores of Buttermere are among the most photographed of any in the Lake District, but this must be one of the earliest pictures. The fells in the background are High Crag and High Stile, with Comb Crags and Burtness Combe in between.

BUTTERMERE, 1889
Looking south down Buttermere from Lower Gatesgarth in 1889. The pines of Crag Wood are prominent in the centre of the photograph, while the slopes of Dodd sweep up the lake shore beyond. Buttermere and Crummock Water were once one large lake, until alluvium from Sail Beck gradually cut it in two.

BUTTERMERE, 1893

Buttermere from Gatesgarth with Whiteless Pike in the background, in 1893. Gatesgarth is a placename which comes from Old Norse language, as do many in the higher hills of the Lake District. It means "the pass where the goats go".

ESTHWAITE WATER, *c.*1900

An Edwardian lady relaxes in a meadow on Colthouse Heights, on the eastern shores of Esthwaite Water, looking across to the knoll of Roger Ground, near Hawkshead, around 1900. Esthwaite Water, south of Hawkshead, is one of the quietest of the lakes, and is a Norse name meaning "the lake by the eastern clearing".

CRUMMOCK WATER, *c.*1893
Whiteless Pike (2,159 ft) is the prominent fell in the view taken from Crummock Water below Mellbreak, with Rannerdale Knotts on the right of the photograph. This picture was taken around 1893 and is virtually unchanged today.

DERWENT WATER and SKIDDAW from Ashness Bridge, 1893
Seen on countless calenders, the view of Derwent Water from Ashness Bridge, on the narrow road up to Watendlath, is always popular. Skiddaw fills the backdrop. Cat Gill is the stream which plunges under the bridge on its way down to meet Derwent Water.

CRUMMOCK WATER from Loweswater, 1889
A picnic party in a meadow in the hamlet of Loweswater enjoying the splendid view north up Crummock Water in 1889. The lower slopes of Grasmoor are prominent on the left and the skyline is filled by Fleetwith Pike, Haystacks and High Crag. Rannerdale Knotts is the small dark hill in the middle distance above the lake.

KESWICK and DERWENT WATER from Latrigg, 1889
The isolated outlier of Latrigg (1,203 ft) is an easy stroll from Keswick and gives a grandstand view of the "capital" of the northern Lakes, as seen in this 1889 photograph. The wooded islands of Derwent, Lord's and St. Herbert's are clearly visible, as are the background Newlands Fells.

Friar's Crag and Causey Pike, DERWENT WATER, 1906
A summer's evening at Friar's Crag on Derwent Water in 1906. This is another of the Lake District's classic viewpoints, the backdrop formed by the peak of Causey Pike (2,035 ft). Friar's Crag is thought to have got its name as the embarkation point from monks visiting St Herbert on his island in the lake.

JOHN·RUSKIN·

·MDCCCXIX + I·MDCCCC·

·THE·FIRST·THING
WHICH·I·REMEMBER
AS·AN·EVENT·IN·LIFE
WAS·BEING·TAKEN·BY
MY·NURSE·TO·THE·BROW
OF·FRIAR'S·CRAG·ON
DERWENT·WATER·

Ruskin Monument, Friar's Crag, DERWENT WATER, 1906
This simple stone obelisk on the summit of Friar's Crag, Derwent Water, commemorates the great Victorian critic and Lake District conservationist John Ruskin, whose early memory was apparently being taken by his nurse to this spot.

Lodore Hotel, DERWENT WATER, 1893
The Lodore Hotel at the southern end of Derwent Water, is a fine Victorian Gothic structure, built at the foot
of the twin cascades, known as the Lodore Falls, which were very popular as a Victorian "sight." The crag in
the background of this 1893 picture is Shepherd's Crag, a popular venue for rock climbers today.

THIRLMERE from Hell How, 1892
This is an historic photograph of Thirlmere, taken from Hell How in 1892. It shows the last of the original two
lakes - Leathe's Water and Wythburn Water - which formerly filled the valley below Helvellyn, but which were
joined and submerged as the Thirlmere Reservoir when Manchester Corporation built the four-mile long
reservoir between 1890-2.

THIRLMERE, 1888
This 1888 view shows the northern end of Thirlmere, looking towards Great How Wood and the Castle Rock of Triermain. Note the young conifers, recently planted in the interest of water purity, which now cloak the artificial lake with their dense canopy of branches.

WASTWATER, 1889
This is one of the classic views of the Lake District – used by the modern National Park Authority as its logo. This 1889 view of the northern shore of Wastwater shows (left to right) the trio of peaks at the head of England's deepest lake – Yewbarrow (2,061 ft), Great Gable (2,949 ft) and Lingmell (2,649 ft).

ULLSWATER from Place Fell, 1892
Ullswater snakes into the Lake District hills for seven and a half miles, from Pooley Bridge to Glenridding, and has three major and quite different stretches. This view looking west from the slopes of Place Fell is towards the head of the lake at Glenridding and shows the northern stretch.

WASTWATER, 1889
A tranquil scene as a rowing boat is moored on the northern shore of Wastwater in 1889. The trees of Low Wood stretch out into the lake, while the steep scree-clad slopes of Illgill Head - the famous Wasdale Screes - soar up the southern shores.

RYDAL WATER, 1886
The peaceful, reed-fringed shores of Rydal Water, near Grasmere, pictured in 1886. Rydal was the home of William Wordsworth from 1813 until his death in 1850, and this was one of his favourite lakes. This well-wooded little lake is now in the hands of the National Trust.

KENDAL

Kendal – "Auld Grey Town" on the River Kent – was founded on the wealth won from the wool of Lakeland sheep. Its motto is *Pannis mihi panis,* which means "wool is my bread" and even Shakespeare refers to Kendal Green cloth in *Henry IV Part 1.* But wool was not Kendal's only industry, and many other trades set themselves up in the many yards which lead off the main street of this modern southern gateway to the Lakes.

KENDAL, 1896
A general view of Kendal from the south on 1896, with the Lakeland hills in the background. The town of Kendal was founded on the west bank of the River Kent, although the earliest settlement around the castle was on the east bank.

Kendal Market, 1926
Kendal was granted the right to hold a market as early as 1189, when it was also made a barony. The Market Place had been enclosed on four sides until 1909, when it was opened to Stricklandgate, from where this 1926 view was taken. It shows the newly unveiled War Memorial in the foreground.

Stricklandgate, KENDAL, 1888
Stricklandgate, the northern extension of Highgate, is one of Kendal's main thoroughfares. The name means "the road leading to the stirk land" and was often referred to as the Drover's Road where cattle were driven from the north. This view was taken in 1888 and shows a traffic-free street looking north.

Nether Bridge, KENDAL, 1914
The lower or Nether Bridge across the River Kent in Kendal, photographed in 1914. Now part of the one-way system, the Nether Bridge links the older, western side of Kendal with the newer, eastern suburbs.

KENDAL, 1896
Miller Bridge, once known as Mill Bridge because it linked the mills on the east of the river with the town, is one of the chief bridges across the River Kent on Kendal. This view taken in 1896 shows the twin spires of the Roman Catholic church beyond.

Grammer School, KENDAL, 1896
Kendal Grammer School, on the banks of the River Kent, photographed in 1896. Just ten years earlier in 1886, the Grammer School had amalgamated with the famous old Blue Coat School, which had itself been founded to prepare boys for the Grammer School in 1670.

KENDAL, 1914
This imposing archway led up a flight of steps to another of Kendal's famous yards, off the main street of Highgate. The use of the word "gate" meaning a road or street, comes from the Old Norse *gata*, and is another clue to the antiquity of the town.

Highgate, KENDAL, 1914

A lad sits on his handcart on the right of this 1914 photograph in a yard off Highgate, Kendal. He appears to be in conversation with a friend seated on the other side of the cobbled yard, while others look on as they pose for the camera.

Stramongate, KENDAL, 1914
This yard, complete with children posed on the steps in the centre, led off Stramongate, the main approach to Kendal from the north-east, from Penrith or Appleby. Stramongate means the "street of the straw men," presumably those who brought the straw to the cattle market.

Rainbow Hotel Yard, KENDAL, 1914

The old coaching inn known as The Rainbow, was one of the many which existed, running off Kendal's main streets since the Middle Ages. The cobbled yard and upper floor gallery is typical of a coaching inn, and once echoed to the sound of horses' hooves as they dashed in through the narrow archway.

Old Gateway, KENDAL, 1914

The datestone above this old archway in Kendal gives its age as 1659. During the seventeenth century, Kendal expanded rapidly as a market town serving the southern part of the Lake District, and this gateway was the one of many which served the yards where the woollen tradesman plied their trade.

New Shambles, KENDAL, 1914
The New Shambles, off Finkle Street, Kendal, was built in 1803. The word "shambles" comes from the Old English *sceamol* which originally meant a bench for the sale of meat, and the New Shambles replaced the Old Shambles, which was on the west side of Highgate. As can be seen in this 1914 photograph many types of shops occupied the units in the New Shambles.

Branthwaite Brow, KENDAL, 1914
Branthwaite Brow is one of the three streets which meet Kent Street, as it leads up the steep hill opposite Miller Bridge in Kendal. The others are Finkle Street and Stramongate. This view looks down Branthwaite Brow towards the River Kent.

THE FELLS AND PASSES

The earliest tourists to the Lake District were overwhelmed by the "horrid" and "frightful" nature of the mountains and crags, which frowned down on them as they negotiated the passes. It was Wordsworth and the other Romantic poets who first instilled the idea that the Lakeland fells had their own beauty and attractions, as generations of walkers and climbers have found since.

Stockley Bridge, Seawaite, BORROWDALE, 1889
Grains Gill tumbles over a series of cascades beneath Stockley Bridge, near Seathwaite in Borrowdale, with Aaron Crags prominent on Seathwaite Fell in the background, in this photograph taken in 1889. The view is hardly changed today.

Skiddaw, near KESWICK, 1889
Snow dusts the shapely, 3,053 ft summit of Skiddaw, the giant among the northern fells, and one of the first popular mountain climbs in the Lake District. The winter view was taken in 1889 from St John's-in-the-Vale and also shows Lonscale Fell to the right.

HONISTER PASS and CRAG, 1889
The great eastern face of Honister Crag dominates the Honister Pass between Borrowdale and Buttermere and Crummock Water, which can be seen in the distance. The Gatesgarthdale Beck flows through the valley. To the left of this 1889 photograph can be seen the workings of the Honister Slate Quarry, which produced some of the finest quality green slate roofing and walling.

Striding Edge, HELVELLYN, 1912
This is one of the classic mountain views in the Lake District, with the glaciated knife-edge of Striding Edge leading off eastwards towards High Spying How from the 3,118 ft summit of Helvellyn, one of the most popular mountains in the Lake District. It is interesting that this 1912 view clearly shows the footpath across the edge, which was obviously being well used even then.

Kirkstone Pass, 1886

A coachman takes a well-earned rest while he waits for fresh horses for his carriage, stopped near the summit of one of the most famous of the Lake District passes, the Kirkstone, which connects Troutbeck and Patterdale. The pass is said to have taken its name from a large rock which looks like the gable end of a church. This view looks south towards Troutbeck, with the shoulder of Broad End on the left.

GREAT GABLE, 1889
This 1889 view of Great Gable is unusual, as it is taken from the north. The usual view of the shapeliest
mountains in the Lake District is from the head of Wasdale, where it dominates the scene. The 2,949 ft summit
has a tablet in memory of the members of the Fell and Rock Climbing Club who died in the First World War.
It was unveiled when the mountain was handed over to the National Trust.

From Green Gable, 1889
The view looking north-west down Ennerdale from Great Gable's sister peak, Green Gable, taken in 1889. Much of this lovely valley is now cloaked under a blanket of coniferous forestry, as are so many of the Lake District dales. The Black Sail Youth Hostel near the head of Ennerdale is one of the most remote in Britain.

LANGDALE PIKE, 1892
The Langdale Pikes are among the Lakeland's most popular and recognisable hills. This view was taken from near the Dungeon Ghyll Hotel, a popular starting point for the hills, in Great Langdale. Stickle Ghyll, which flows down from Stickle Tarn, passes under the bridge in this 1892 view looking towards the 2,403 ft summit of Harrison Stickle, the highest of the pikes.

Striding Edge and Red Tarn, HELVELLYN, 1912
Another view from Nethermost Pike, Helvellyn in 1912, showing the waters of Red Tarn in its glaciated corrie and the sweeping ridge of Striding Edge in the foreground, leading round to High and Low Spying How and Bleaberry Crag in the distance.

GRASMERE VALE, 1926
Not much traffic – a car and a motorcycle with pillion passenger – in this 1926 view of the road running down from Dunmail Raise into Grasmere. The lake and village of Grasmere can be seen in the distance, while to the right, the "Lion and Lamb" summit rocks of Helm Crag are seen silhouetted against the skyline

LITTLE LANGDALE, 1888
This 1888 view from Little Langdale looks towards Langdale Pikes, with the thimble-shaped Pike 'o' Stickle (2,323 ft) prominent on the left, and Gimmer Crag, and Harrison Stickle (2,403 ft) on the right in the distance. The slopes of Blake Rigg rise towards the left of the photograph.

GREAT LANGDALE, 1888
Pike 'o' Stickle (2,323 ft) is the thimble-shaped peak prominent on the skyline in this 1888 view taken from near the head of Great Langdale. In the scree slope just visible below the summit of Pike 'o' Stickle, a prehistoric axe factory was discovered, where the hard volcanic tuff was shaped into axes and transported all over Britain.

PILLAR ROCK, 1889
The west face of Pillar Rock in Ennerdale, taken in 1889. Pillar Rock is one of the most impressive rock features in the Lake district, and was a favourite place for rock climbing in the district by some of the early pioneers of the sport, such as O.G. Jones and the Abraham brothers, at about the time this photograph was taken.

Pictorial Memories Collection

A great new range of publications featuring the work of innovative Victorian photographer Francis Frith.

FRITH PUBLISHING, WATERTON ESTATE, BRIDGEND, GLAMORGAN, CF31 3XP.

TEL: 01656 668836   FAX: 01656 668710

1-84125 *Themed Poster Books*   £4.99

000-7	Canals and Waterways	
001-5	High Days and Holidays	
003-1	Lakes and Rivers	
004-x	Piers	
005-8	Railways	
044-9	Ships	
002-3	Stone Circles & Ancient Monuments	
007-4	Tramcars	

Town & City Series   £9.99

010-4	Brighton & Hove	
015-5	Canterbury	
012-0	Glasgow & Clydeside	
011-2	Manchester	
040-6	York	

Town & City series Poster Books   £5.99

018-x	Around Brighton	
023-6	Canterbury	
043-0	Derby	
020-1	Glasgow	
011-2	Manchester	
041-4	York	

County Series   £9.99

024-4	Derbyshire	
028-7	Kent	
029-5	Lake District	
031-7	Leicestershire	
026-0	London	
027-9	Norfolk	
030-9	Sussex	
025-2	Yorkshire	

County Series Poster Books   £4.99

032-5	Derbyshire	
036-8	Kent	
037-6	Lake District	
039-2	Leicestershire	
034-1	London	
035-x	Norfolk	
038-4	Sussex	
033-3	Yorkshire	

Available
soon

County Series   £9.99

045-7	Berkshire	
053-8	Buckinghamshire	
055-4	East Anglia	
077-5	Greater London	
051-1	Lancashire	
047-3	Staffordshire	
049-x	Warwickshire	
063-5	West Yorkshire	

County Series Poster Books   £4.99

046-5	Berkshire	
054-6	Buckinghamshire	
056-2	East Anglia	
078-3	Greater London	
052-x	Lancashire	
048-1	Staffordshire	
050-3	Warwickshire	
064-3	West Yorkshire	

Country Series   £9.99

075-9	Ireland	
071-6	North Wales	
069-4	South Wales	
073-2	Scotland	

Country Series Poster Books   £4.99

076-7	Ireland	
072-4	North Wales	
070-8	South Wales	
074-0	Scotland	

A selection of our 1999 programme:
County Series and Poster Books
Devon, Cornwall, Essex,
Nottinghamshire, Cheshire.

Town and City Series and Poster Books
Bradford, Edinburgh, Liverpool, Nottingham,
Stamford, Bristol, Dublin,
Stratford-upon-Avon, Bath, Lincoln,
Cambridge, Oxford, Matlock, Norwich.

Themed Poster Books
Castles, Fishing, Cricket, Bridges, Cinemas,
The Military, Cars.